The Alchemy of Mind

Poems

In these poems Flamur Vehapi sings
from his heart the gift of life, the joys and sorrows,
challenges and opportunities,
and the love that brings us together.
—Bob Valine,
editor of *The Second Birth* and writing instructor at
Rogue Community College

"Flamur's poetry reveals both the tragedy
of his past and his hope for the future.
Peace, love and acceptance are evident
among his beautiful messages."
—Jerry Kenefick,
president of *Rotary Club of
Ashland Lithia Springs*

THE ALCHEMY OF MIND

Poems

FLAMUR VEHAPI

To order additional copies of this book, contact:
Xlibris Corporation
1-888-795-4274
www.Xlibris.com
Orders@Xlibris.com
52643

To my beloved parents,
my sister, brother and his wife
and Blendi

To everyone in Kosova
and in the United States of America
who has helped me
to get where
I am

Good poetry . . . makes the universe . . . reveal its . . . 'secret.'

—Hafiz[1]

For all footnotes, please see *Quotations, Inspirations and Other Notes* at the end of this book.

Contents

III.

IV.

V.

Acknowledgements

First of all, I am thankful that the Almighty Creator gave me the ability to think, read and write. Secondly, I can never adequately express my thanks to everyone who has supported me in writing this book of poetry. Many thanks to my family for their support, especially to my mother who, since my early age, encouraged me to get an education during times of hardship. She has diligently encouraged me to study English since I was twelve. As a result of her support, today I am publishing my second book, and translating some of my Albanian poems into English.

Thanks to Mr. Joseph DioGuardi, the former U.S. Congressman, and Shirley Cloyes DioGuardi, Balkan Affair Advisor, for all their support. Special thanks to Linda Barnes, Rick Williams, Doyne Mraz, Greg Marton, Bob Valine, Jane Brockman, Colin Mills-Cannon, Kori Bieber and Peter Angstadt from Rogue Community College for all their help and support. The following deserve a special note of thanks: Carl and Donna, Richard and Ann Offenbacher; Bob and Phyllis Johns; Linda and Mike Tresemer; Marisa and Gary Petersen; Gustav and Lynne Schefstrom; also Harvey and Evelyn Seeley. A very special thank-you to the following families: Manlulu and Rockholt, Jones, Maralusha, Solomita, Sours, Bryan, Glass, McDonald, Brazeau, and many more.

Many thanks to the following: Florim Krasniqi, for the permission to use his remarkable drawing on the cover of my book; Mike Frye and Edward Reed for the cover design; and egyptcollections. com for the permission to use their Kyamya image on the cover of this book.

Thank you to all the Rogue Community College and Southern Oregon University students, professors and faculty members for encouraging me to bring these poems to light today for the first time in the United States of America.

Comments on this book may be addressed to author at fvehapi@gmail.com.

About the Author

Flamur Vehapi was born in 1984 in a small village called Suhadoll, near the town of Lipjan in Kosova. He studied there until 1992 when the regime of the Serbian dictator, Slobodan Milošević, ordered the closing of all the schools for the Kosovar Albanians in their homelands. Even though it was illegal at that time for Albanian students to pursue education, he still continued his schooling while hiding from the Serbian military forces and even local civilians. When the war began and his home, as well as the whole village, was set on fire by some Serbian soldiers, Flamur, together with his family, was a refugee of war joining over a million other countrymen from Kosova. With his family, he had the opportunity to escape to Macedonia and then was transferred to Italy with the help of Italian NATO troops. He continued his education there and shortly afterwards moved to Switzerland in search of better opportunities. When the war ended in Kosova, the Vehapis returned home. In 2003, Flamur graduated from high school and enrolled at the University of Prishtina in Kosova to study English Language and Literature. Three years ago, he had the opportunity to come to America in pursuit of education. On June 14, 2008, he graduated from Rogue Community College and now is attending Southern Oregon University in Ashland, Oregon. He is majoring in psychology with minors in history and international studies. Flamur lives in Southern Oregon.

Introduction

Flamur knows how to listen. When you meet him, he listens to you with his entire being, standing poised and calm, taking in everything before he responds. His mind is quick, yet his motions are deliberate and patient. He radiates kindness.

How can this be so? We have many theories about how children exposed to traumatic situations, such as war, turn out to be broken and troubled adults. In Flamur's case, quite the opposite happened. From his painful childhood emerged a young man intent on bringing healing and insight into the world. How can we show enough gratitude for such a gift?

I love nothing better than to have Flamur visit my classroom and to share his story with my American students. People of all ages respond with awe and respect to his story. Now his poetry is here to further inspire and delight us.

In these pages, the reader can peek into the mind and heart of an extraordinary being. Inspired by Hafiz, Rumi, and other poets and philosophers, with his own brand of humor and occasional irony, Flamur brings insights into our common humanity. When so much of the world seems intent upon dividing us from one another, this message of unity, peace and wonder is all too rare.

If you ever meet Flamur in person, you will know that these poems reflect with honest truth his compassionate view of life. I hope you do get the chance to meet him, and experience his deep listening. Until then, it is your turn to listen.

By Linda Barnes
Medford, Oregon

—*I*—

Really we create nothing.
We merely plagiarize nature.

—Jean Baitaillon[2]

The Alchemy of Mind

Treasure of our being
Melting down the hills
And valleys all around,
Flowing into the brain
Through the gates of mind,
It filters through life
And finally comes together
In one body of light.

Let it Rain

Mercy from the heavens
Drops on earth
Reviving it
And blessing it
With a new life.

I stand in the rain
Feeling its coolness
From its journey
With all my heart
Until my tears
Mingle with it
Then I walk away
And let it rain.

Let it rain until
The heavens drain,
So let it rain.

Enlightment from Nature

The world is full of lessons,
Everywhere you look
You see a teacher,
And everything you hear
Speaks a message,
And whatever you touch
Shares its secret.

Nature gives wisdom
To those who listen.

Right now,
As the stream flows
And the rocks roll
Through the pure water
There is a calming sound
That teaches peace
Within our hearts.[3]

Look and See

Look you, look
What a wonderful world
We live in.
We humans exceed
Every living creature
On this globe.

We are granted
The best gifts
Of all times,
But look at you,
Look how much
You appreciate,
Look.

#

Sing, sing you birds
With that lovely voice
Coming from your hearts.

Sing and rejoice
Every morning
All day long
Because each dawn
New life begins.

Sing from sunrise
Until sunset
Because tomorrow
You don't know
If you'll wake up.
Sing!

ream

Dream about today,
The near future
And the far one.

Dream,
For dreams are steps
That help you
Conquer the hills
Of the road ahead.

Dream,
Day and night
Never stop dreaming,
For dreams are
Paving stones
That smooth your way
To the success
Of your future.

Keep in mind
Without dreams
You are dead.

Dream,
But also remember
To wake up one day
And make those dreams
Come true
Then go back again
And dream.

From Earth on Earth

The Earth,
A giant creature
In the solar system . . .

Seed of humankind
And bed to everyone
And everything
Living on the ground
And flying in the sky.

Earth,
Home to everyone,
And like a breadbasket
Feeding us all.
Unfortunately one day,
And we know for sure,
You and I will be its bread,
Adding another layer to earth,
Combined with mud.

. . . Earth, as small as
A grain of sand,
Within this universe.

A Mirror of Life

Looking out the window
For a little sunshine
On this mid winter day
And I see nothing
But myself
On a broken glass
Hanging like a mirror.

An Art of Peace

During the enjoyable days
And the bitter ones,
When life gets arduous,
All you can do
Is breathe.

Breathe in and absorb
The whole universe
With all its marvels.

Then easily breathe out
Letting your breath
Become part of the universe.

Keep breathing in and out
During hardship and ease
Working diligently
To live the Art of Peace.[4]

The Underwater World

Covered down there
Where we didn't think of,
In wide blue oceans
Deep down in the sea,
Places no human eye had seen
And no mind had conceived
Exists another world,
Which speaks a foreign language
Practices different cultures
And follows various traditions.

Now, I know for a fact
There is a world down there
Joyful and amused,
That dances and sings
Morning, noon and night
Rejoicing in celebration
Of its diverse creation,
Yet the human ear is deaf
To hear any of that melody
Of their universal integrity. [5]

The Future of Nature

The nature we know
Was once born
And beautified
With pure blue seas
And green vegetations
On the fertile soil,
And humankind
Was appointed
As its steward
For the ages to come.

Assuredly,
The nature we know
Will come to an end
Like it came to being,
So lets work together
To slow down the aging
Of this parent-like nurturer.

Unfortunately,
The future of nature
And that of civilizations,
Sadly enough to know,
Greatly depends on us.[6]

Unite

All I am asking
Is to unite the colors
Of the earth
With those of the sky.

You don't have to blend
In order to survive,
For even the colors
Of the gleamy rainbow
Never quite blend
But together in peace
Vividly and proudly
They all stand.

Tonight

Looking at the stars
Of this endless universe
On this solitary night,
Quiet and dark,
I think of you,
Only of you,
The sparkling star
Amidst other stars,
Anxiously waiting
To hear your voice
But no, you are not near,
Waiting to hear a word
But you are not here.
Tonight, like every night,
I think of you
And write about you
In the brightness
Of the lonely moon,
Thinking about you,
Where are you!

I Am Here

Sitting by the riverbank
Watching the ducks swim
Lined up one after the other
I sense myself
Feeling I am not here,
Feeling like in a dream,
But no, I know I am here,

It is you who is missing
In this real picture
That I just framed.

Your Name

I think I am ready
To arrange the stars
For you,
And write your name
With them in the sky.

Time and Space

Twin concepts
Heading different directions
Apart from one another,
Yet through "worldlines"
They both meet
At the same point,
Interwoven together
Creating spacetime.[7]

Imagine

Imagine a garden
Full of vegetables
Surrounded by fences,
Yet it has no gardener.

Imagine an engine
That runs every second
Making our lives easier,
Yet it is without an engineer.

Imagine a book
That contains knowledge
To educate a nation,
Yet it is without an author

Imagine a world
Full of beautiful creatures
Sustaining them all,
Yet many of them say
"It has no Creator."

Imagine the planets
Traveling around
The solar system,
Yet there is no sun.

Imagine!

—*II*—

Only during hard times do people come to understand how difficult it is to be master of their feelings and thoughts.

—Anton Chekhov[8]

The Tempests of Life

This is the way they are,
The tempests of this life,
Often leaving the abominable
And taking the pleasing with them. [9]

A Journey Back in Time

Looking at the sky
Illuminated by stars,
This quiet night
Brought to my mind
Some old memories
Mixed with tears,
Some memories
Mingled with fears.
The mind itself recalls
The wailing history
Written on muddy lanes
By refugees' tracks,
Escaping their homes
Groggy and barefoot,
Crying and glancing back
From time to time,
Making sure that death
Is still a few feet away.

Oh, monstrous days
Please make nobody
Go through that misery
And agony again,
Never again, never.

 So Did I

I did see those days too,
The days with no light,
Dimmed in darkness
Splashed with blood.

I saw those atrocious days
Horrific, unfortunate
Wicked and bereaving,
Viciously astounding.

The dawn was frightening
Coming like a python,
And the sunshine descending
With an entombed light.

Ruthless was the night,
And bloody like a sword,
Lengthy was the nighttime
Gulping those in their beds.[10]

Did You Want to Know?

Did you want to know
Who I am, my friend,
And where I come from?
Did you really want
To hear my story,
The story that I wrote
With roses grown on blood?
But I tell you now,
It is not going to be easy
For me to tell it
Nor for you to listen.

The days I survived
Held no mercy for me
Nor for my people,
Whose blood was spilled,
And their bodies disappeared
With no explanation.
Did you truly want
To hear my words
That I don't want
To repeat
With memories of war,
Fear and terror?

I know you want
To hear my voice,
But I tell you then
There was no voice,
There were no sounds
Except the noises
Of the rampant guns
And the loud voices
Of crying mothers
For their fallen
Members of the heart.

In case you wanted more
To know about that land,
Please don't ask me
But ask the history,
Written by human blood
On human skulls
Found in Kosova.

Did you really want
To hear anymore,
Did you really?[11]

A Golden Rule

The universal Golden Rule
Descended from heaven
For all beings
Living on earth,
Yet, who lives by it?
All but humans.

We broke it into pieces
And made our own
"golden rules,"
Imposing them
On the others,
By "preaching"
And force,
Proudly saying
"Welcome to the 'true'
golden rules."

This Is Our World

Every single morning
Waking up thankful,
I watch the news,
And I see nothing else
But bloodshed,
Hatred and fighting,
You might wonder
Between who and who.
No, not us versus aliens
But us versus us.

Men, women and children
Covered in blood,
And the rest around them
Bathed in tears.

This is our world,
Big enough for all,
No need for some
To live in fear,
Persecution and death,
Because this is our world.

Siblings against siblings
Sucking each other's blood
With no mercy or shame,
And one may ask "why?"

Because we have forgotten
Who we really are.

Men, women and children
Covered in blood,
And the rest around them
Don't bother to care.

Ah, Adam and Eve, look,
Look what has become
Of your children today!

Freedom

(For Kosova)

I know that freedom
Is a joy of life,
I know that freedom
Is an ingredient
Of human existence,
But I also know
That often times
It is expensive
And can't be found
On market stands.

Sometimes it costs a lot,
Some few cannot afford it,
Some pay for it with their lives.

Some might ask:
"How do you know?"
And some may ask,
"What do you know?"
I do not really know
Much about freedom
But surviving without it,
And living in agony
I can tell about freedom
That my people never had.

Truly, "freedom is
The oxygen of the soul,"[12]
"So let freedom ring"[13]
In order for people to breathe.

Forgiveness

My dear friend
Do not ever say
"I can't forgive,"
Please don't tell me
That you can't.

Are you saying
You can't erase the past?
And are you saying
You can't forgive the guilty
And not turn the other cheek?

As I know, we are all one;
Each and every one of us
Does wrong in this life,
And none of us is pure
As we like to be.

Please do not tell me
That you can't forgive.

I forgave my freedom's thief
I forgave my enemy,
And do you think
That it was so easy?

Sure, you can do it
You can forgive the past,
And open your eyes
By looking forward
To unveil the future.

But just don't say
That you can't.
Please do not tell me that.

To Our Greedy Eyes

How interesting
Are human beings.
You give them a river
They ask you for a sea,
You give them the sea
They ask for an ocean.

And if you ask them
For a cup of water
Out of that ocean,
They will make you wish
You had not asked for it.

Yes, Montaigne got it right when he said
That our eyes are bigger than our stomachs.[14]

ar

(For Kosova and Bosnia)

War
A great chunk
Of bloody bones
Piled up
On a burned land . . .

War
Who knows better
What it means
Than the parents
Of the fallen children?
Who knows better
Than the children
Of the fallen parents?

War
A cursed cause
On a burned land,
Saturated in blood,
And abandoned by birds.[15]

Can't We All Live Together?

Scions of Adam,
Sons and daughters of Eve,
Raised in the same cradle
And fed from the same dish,
Took different paths.

After ages of separation
Today they come together,
But in hope of celebration
I see nothing more than devastation.

Stunned by the fratricide
And heartbroken in horror,
I remind myself of advice
That once a learned one said:
"We must learn to live together
as brothers or perish together as fools."[16]

Excuses

No excuse for us
To repeat the past,
For we grow up
Making mistakes,
And at some point
We should learn
To avoid mischief
Upon the face of earth.

After so many years
Of trial and error
There is no excuse
For repeating the past,
Because the future
Doesn't have time
To wait
For you and me,
But it simply goes,
With the flow.

Universal Integrity

Even the brainless planets,
Particles in this galaxy,
Circle around humbly
In a slow and quiet motion
Floating in the universe
And never colliding
With one another.

Each time they pass by one another
They spin around, and smile,
And when they leave they cry
For their spinning ring lovers.

This should be a great example
For the clashing humanity to learn
The way of moving together
Towards the Great Universal Integrity. [17]

—*III*—

*A poem begins in delight and
ends in wisdom.*

—Robert Frost[18]

An Age of Great Transformations

Now,
Like never before,
Humans are
Closer
To each other.

Now,
Like never before,
Life has invited us
To dance together
In this Golden Age,
Never lived before
By any terrestrial.

Now,
It is time to love,
And unite our souls,
Holding hands
And dancing,
Dance flying
Into the silver gates
Of the future.

Other Worlds

Maybe there are worlds
Out there in the heavens
That I still can't see,
With strange people
Like you and me.

Maybe there are worlds
That heavens hide
From human eyes,
And human reasons.

Maybe there are people
That we can't understand,
But it makes no difference
Since we don't even understand
Each other here
Living on the same planet,
Or in the same neighborhood.

Maybe there are other worlds
That we are not supposed to see,
Or maybe there are worlds
But we close our eyes
And refuse to see.

Prisoners of the Self

O, prisoners,
Self-prisoned,
Open the iron gates
That you have built
Around you
And free yourselves
From your own prisons.

Be free, and run freely,
Run until you reach
True freedom of mind.

A Nobody That Became Somebody

Once upon a time
There was a Nobody
Created miraculously
Out of a drop of water
On a site of mud.

Then this poor Nobody
Became a proud "Somebody"
Once was humble,
Now a mischief-maker
Disobeying, arrogant
And an oath breaker,
Not realizing that one day
Like particles of ash
He will be blown away.

And when you ask
"Where is that Somebody?"
Meekly they will answer
"He was Nobody."

Some Days

There are some days
When I want to rest,
Be quiet and listen
To the beats of the heart
And hear others
What they have to say
About this small world.

There are some days
Quiet in my heart
When I don't feel like
Doing anything at all
But closing my eyes
And hearing my heart.

Just closing my eyes
And listening to my mind,
Trying to unwire those neurons
That attract me so much
To covet this world,
The world that doesn't belong to me,
Or to anyone else on earth.

Some Human Creation

Since we came to being
This quiet nature
Has "threatened" us
Throughout the ages,
By trying to adopt
Through its cycle changes
But watch today,
It is the other way around
We threaten nature
With our proud creation
That more easily
Can lead to destruction
And even self-devastation.

In Someone Else's Shoes

It is easy to judge
When you are not judged,
And you can easily mock
When you are not mocked.

It should not be hard to accept
If you have been rejected,
You can't easily forget
If you have ever been forgotten.

But if you have never fallen
From a very tall tree,
You can't really tell
What that feels like.

I See Them

I see people on the street
Walking, talking and smiling,
The others say "hi" and leave
And I never see them again.

I see friends and families
Getting together on weekends,
To meet with one another,
The next hour they all disperse.

I see those who love each other
And those who hate themselves,
Complaining and never smiling
Like someone who is about to die.

I see those who can help the needy
Even if they share five cents a day
But they don't do it
Because they fear
Going bankrupt.

I see hope, I see the people
Who can change the world
With love and acceptance,
Work and dedication,
But right now we are too busy,
Occupied by the life of this world.

December 21, 2012?

What does it matter
If the end of days
Is sooner or later,
Today, tomorrow
Or the day after tomorrow?
Surely, I can't pause it,
Rewind or fast forward it,
Or even escape from it,
But wait eagerly
For the bell to ring.

Just like any of us,
I took no part
In this creation,
Neither did the Maya.
And it is not my position
To make any speculation
About the world's destination.

But one thing is for sure,
One day in the near future
"The Hour will come,
There can be no doubt, about it."[19]

And certainly,
The One who creates
Is the only One
Who terminates.

On Maturation

There are those
Who grow in maturity
Since their childhood,
And there are those
Who grow old
And immature
Throughout their adulthood.

The significance of this
Is that neither one of those
Knows these characteristics
About themselves.

All About Them

For so many centuries
We called ourselves
The center of the universe,
Ignoring the truth
Outside our walls,
Until Scientific Revolution
Made us wear glasses
Enabling us to see clearly
The true nature
Of the universe.

Today, shortly after,
Many think they are
The center of the universe
Ignoring those around them.
And everything they do
Is all about them,
For them and by them.

It is all about them.

Let It Be?

If I see broken glass
In my path
I am not going
To ignore it,
Nor jump over it,
And walk away
To let it be.

I am going to change it,
Clear it out of the way,
To make it safe
For those who come after me.

Don't let it be,
Let's fix things,
Then walk away
And let them be.

Taking the Time

He who initiates
Is brave and courageous,
He who takes action
Is brave too
In his own way,
But the bravest of both
Is he who observes
And records both,
Initiation and action,
While remaining calm
And patient, in silence,
Noting the results.

Walking by Myself

Walking through the streets alone
Pushing the fallen leaves aside
I open myself a way
To the gateways of mind.

And every step I take
I think of my companion
Who isn't by my side
And I ask myself the question
That Lao Tsu had asked
A long, long time ago
"Can the gate to Yin be open
without inviting Yang?"[20]

—*IV*—

The art of living is more like wrestling than dancing.

—Markus Aurelius[21]

Internal Forces

There are internal forces
Within our bodies
Like two sumos
Pushing on each other
In a struggle for victory.

They fall and rise,
Roll and stand
But never give up.

They live and grow
Together in our bodies
Being fed by us.

If we feed one
More than the other
The scale moves
Making us lose control
Of human balance.

Controlling the Self

Those who can't control themselves
Are no different than animals,
For there are even some animals
That think twice before taking action.

The old Taoist master
Once said to his people
Those who control themselves
Have uncommon inner strength,[22]
And surely those who don't
Are inviting disaster.

The inner self is powerful indeed,
It can change human direction,
Even easily cause our downfall,
Depending on the way we drive it.

Certainly, those are courageous
Who struggle to control themselves
Instead of others.

And the prophet once said
"The most excellent struggle
Is that for the conquest of self."[23]

A Changing World

I remember the sun shinning
During the warm seasons,
It did,
But not anymore.

I recall the moon
Lighting my window
Before I went to sleep,
It used to,
But not anymore.

I remember you also
Smiling and laughing
A long time ago,
But not anymore.

I recall the sun shinning
During the flower seasons,
It certainly did,
But not anymore,
At least not like before.

A Timed Life

Time goes by
As we now breathe,
Days run fast
One after the other,
Leaving behind
Human footsteps
That came yesterday,
Live today,
And will die tomorrow.

Time goes fast
And as you live
Use it wisely,
Never let it use you.

As long as I breathe
I won't let time
Make me part
Of cosmic disorder.

The Present

The present moment
Of your exquisite life
Is a great product
Of your past.

Now, the past is over
You are living the present
And this present time
Is a slow approach
To the boarding station
Of your future.

The Future

Past and present
Both build on each other
Like the stories
Of ancient civilizations.

Past and present
Are the cornerstones
Of the future,
So be careful
Where you get
Those stones,
How you carve them
As foundations
For this new building.

A Hidden Treasure

Walking the earth
I climb the mountains
Searching in caves
And holes in the ground,
Scanning the waters
And the ocean basins
Looking for clues
That would lead to a treasure,
The treasure of the future.

I decide to rest
Taking a deep breath
Then suddenly remember
What Rumi had said:
" . . . if you want to find
the greatest treasure
Don't look outside,
Look inside . . ."[24]

I Trust in Human Capacity

I believe humans
Can truly
Change the world
For good
If we all
Embrace each other,
As we are,
For who people are,
Live and work
As one, together,
Until the trumpet blows.

Life Has Many Shapes

Through the years
After we are born
Life builds a box
Around us.

The head and body
Get stuck inside
While our limbs
Remain out
Just to let us move.

This box is big,
Strong and stable
Yet invisible.

The huge box
Is a burden
Since while in our box
We can't pass
Through circular
Or triangular doors
Of this life
Of countless shapes.

Wait,
I think I just got out
Of this hard box,
But how do I stay
Out of it?
That, I am still working on.[25]

I Am Who You See

Many that I met
Have more than a face
And some other ones
Have sacks full of them,
For everyone they come across
They put on a new face,
And continue to exist proudly
Living a faceless life.

Many times I ponder,
Sometimes I am afraid
That some may assume
I am one of them,
And my heart is not out
For them to see what's in it.

I want them to know
That I truly am
The person they see.

The End of Lives

Life is admirable,
It is a miracle
For those who know it.

But, unfortunately one day
Our precious lives
Will come to an end
Whether we are ready or not.

Eventually one moment,
Sooner or later,
We will all meet death,
Another friend of ours,
Another part of our lives.

However,
Death is nothing but a bridge
Between this life and the afterlife,
So don't worry about death,
But get ready for the new journey
Into the Hereafter.

Fear of Failure

We all fear
Sometimes
This byzantine life
That threatens us
Everyday
With failure.
Therefore,
Most of us act weak
In face of it
Because the others
Tell us to.

I believe that to be
Nothing more
Than a hegemonic myth
That can't make me
Change my course
Away from the bright future
Waiting ahead.

However, a great teacher said,
"Our greatest glory
Is not in never falling
But in rising every time we fall."[26]

What if Life Is a Dream?

"Living" all the wonders
On this golden age
What if life is a dream?
How would I feel
If the alarm went off
And I had to wake up
Open my eyes
And look all around me
Seeing none but myself,
How would I feel?
Running and running
Into an endless space
No light or voice,
How would I feel?
Where would I go?
What would you do?
Where would you go?
Probably back to sleep.

The Missing Smiles

Streets full of people,
Running in different directions,
On many various paths,
To-ing and fro-ing
Like the honeybees.

They all breathe,
They all move,
But none looks pleased.

And as I walk
I ask myself
"Do they all think
They will live forever?"

Cheer up! Laugh!
You are here today,
And tomorrow
You may not be.

Tides of Life

Truly
There can't be light
Without darkness,
Nor darkness
Without light,
For these two
Always go together,
There can't be one
Without the other
And when they clash
Into each other
They don't fall apart
But harmoniously
They mingle together
Creating a balance
That Lao Tsu called
Yin and Yang.

—*V*—

We are shaped and fashioned by what we love.

—Johann Wolfgang von Goethe[27]

I Think I Know

I know what it is
To live in loneliness,
I know what it means
To have your shade
As a companion,
And I truly know
That I am not
The only one.

I realize the pain
Of life in darkness,
Where the only sounds
Are my own heartbeats
And the echoes of my breath
But at the same time,
I humbly accept
That I am not alone,
Even though
It may seem so.

I know there is One,
Here and there
Who knows all
That I don't know.

There is One
Watching closely
What I think and do,
One that lightens the way,
And shields me
Every second
Of my existence.

I know, I admit,
I am not alone,
In this selfish world.

His Wisdom

Only He knows
Everything,
The possible
And the 'impossible.'
He knows everything
On the left
And on the right,
Upwards and downwards,
Past, present and future
Because He created
All the existing,
All endless universe
Adorned with stars,
And He was, is and will be
The Owner of all
Until the end of days.

The Source of All Light

As a child
I used to speculate
Like the ancients,
Reasoning
That the strong
And shining angels
Brought down
The light to earth,
But now I know
That even the angels
Are weak and dark
Without the True Source of Light.

Possessions

With all these miracles
That I possess today,
That I never had before
I am truly afraid
That I will forget
That I possess nothing,
Not even my body,
Nor even my soul.

Creation

I look out in nature
To find some evidence
Of the Creator
In His creation
Completely forgetting
That I myself
Am the first creation
To start with.

A Prophet

Centuries ago
During a time of chaos
And confusion on earth,
An orphan was born.

Living in a desert,
Illiterate and poor,
Through struggle and suffering
He became a man.

Living as a shepherd,
In solitude and prayer,
He was embraced by light
And given the Message.

For years to come
His ascetic, humble life
And his enlightening words
Forever reshaped the stream
Of human thought.

Yet, he is ignored.[28]

A Message

The Divine Word
Was given to him
For a heavy mission
To flow on earth
That even the mountains
Could not have handled.

He trembled at first
When words were revealed
But as the chain continued
He nailed them in his heart.

This Magnificent Word
That came through the heavens
Was given to all humanity,
And is a mercy for us
A healer for bodies,
A freedom for minds,
And a unifier of souls.

Read!

Coming and Leaving

I came into this world
Without anything,
All naked.
Later in time
I do my best
To gain something,
The necessities of this life.
After getting what I deserve
I get ready to leave
This world,
Again
Without anything.

Yes, You Can

It truly hurts
Deep in this heart
Hearing some say:
"That's the end of it,
I think I should just quit."

These are the people
Of the spoiled generation
Who are heedless
Of the power of imagination.

They don't even realize
That those who succeed
Are no more than human.

When you take a journey
Be prepared to face hurdles,
And always keep walking
Because no wall
Is impassable.

Remember what a teacher said:
"Even the least one of you
Can do all that I have done,
And even greater."[29]

Yes, you can!

On Love

To be born means to live
To live means to learn,
To live and learn means to love
To love means to unite
Both body and soul.

To love is acceptance and justice
Honesty and integrity,
That makes up the wholeness,
The circle of eternity.

Love is not just a word
But a divine rule here
Linked to the Other World.

To love means two equals one.

A True Alchemist

An alchemist
Can be a person
Who turns minerals
Into gold
For his own profit,
But a true alchemist
Is a person
Who turns his words
And his promises
Into action
For the benefit
Of others,
For the greater good.

Mornings for You

Every morning
When the sunshine
Penetrates
My windows
It brings you
To my mind.

When I open
The window,
The clear air
Refreshes me
With thoughts
Of you.

Every morning comes,
And of course
Every morning goes
But only you,
You stay forever
In my mind.

I Thought

I thought I would never write a love poem again
But tonight I broke the promise given to myself.

I also believed that poetry was a waste of time
But tonight I changed my mind, only because of you.

I decided to write, whatever comes to my mind,
Yet, nothing comes to my mind but you.

Modesty

Like a mirror,
Human modesty
Truly reflects
The interior image
Of a person's heart.

The prophet said
"True modesty is
the source of all virtue."[30]
And I believe
The modest,
Through peace
And silence,
Smoothly
Keep life rolling.

Heavens without Pillars

I wonder in the morning
And wonder at night,
About the heavens
Above my head,
That I certainly
Have no knowledge of.

The stars, the moon
And the sun that I see,
They all stand quietly
As if they had pillars
Holding them strong,
Yet I see none.

I am standing
On this oval shape
That is not tied
Nor placed
On anything,
Yet I am secure,
Am I?

There is no way I'll die
And not send my thanks
To the Maker of Order,
The Watchful One.

Just Another Pilgrim

Waking up in the morning
Realizing that I am alive,
I gratefully start the day
Like a bee from its hive.

Jumping flower to flower
In search of truth and light
Meekly seeking knowledge
Morning, noon and night.

Hoping to live this life
As humbly as I can
Knowing that in this world
Nothing but a pilgrim I am.[31]

One ought, every day at least, to hear a little song, read a good poem, see a fine picture and, if possible, speak a few reasonable words.

—Johann Wolfgang von Goethe[32]

A Note from the Author

I remember when I was twelve reading the writings of some of the greatest Albanian poets of the nineteenth and twentieth centuries that truly sparked in me the desire to write. Since then, I have always written poems and prose, usually sharing them with my family members and friends at school back in Kosova. I have always been fascinated with those writers who published their numerous books. It became my dream to publish my writings one day, too.

After reading some of my poems to my family, my mother suggested to my uncle the idea that I should publish my poems; he had previously published one of his books of poetry. Immediately afterwards, my uncle spoke to me and said he was ready to help me with editing and publishing. At that point, my excitement went as high as it could get. Since then, I was determined to publish my book of poetry.

As years passed, the situation got worse and worse in Kosova. Like any Kosovar Albanian student, I too lost my school as a second grader in 1992. From that time on, most of the Kosovar Albanian students received an education secretly. All the schools that we had shared with the Serbian students were closed for the Albanians. As a result of the hard political and economic situation, many Kosovar Albanians who left Kosova were kind to let us use their houses as private schools. My siblings, family members, friends and I studied in those "schools" for almost eight years. There were no conditions for education at all, but we had no other choice. What is worse, even when we went to those schools, we couldn't tell anyone on the street where we were going, especially the Serbs. Education for Albanians was illegal, according to the regime of Slobodan Milošević; however, we never obeyed his law imposed on us. I recall going to school and groups of Serbian kids, most of the time encouraged by their parents, stopping us in the middle of the road, making us return home, most of the time by force. We would go home and cry to our parents. Even worse than that, we weren't able to complain to anyone or prevent this from happening because there were no institutions protecting the human rights of the Albanian people in Kosova. According to the regime of that time, an Albanian was equal to an animal; however, sometimes animals had *more* rights than we.

By 1997, the situation was getting worse in many areas of Kosova. That was the year when the first sparks of war appeared throughout the country, especially in the region of Drenica, central Kosova. Even then, my friends and I still risked in going to school and getting the education we longed for. Year 1998 was known as the year of guns and fire. Many Albanians were forced to flee their homes and find shelter, going wherever life was less dangerous. At that time, my family and I were still living in the village where our great-grandfather had lived. We wanted to escape from the country but didn't know where to go, or how. Unfortunately, we Albanians were isolated however one looked at it. Escape was difficult, and even if there were a way to escape, our hope in the United States and the United Nations kept us waiting anxiously for their intervention.

Not until March 24, 1999, did this dream come true. That day, after thousands of people had been killed, the NATO alliance began bombing Yugoslavian military bases all over Yugoslavia as a way to bring an end to the war in Kosova. However, this did not immediately stop the shedding of the Albanian blood. I remember my father telling my family the Serbs in the next village had said to him, "If NATO bombs us, we kill you (Albanians)," and that is exactly how they went about it.

While NATO aircraft were bombing the Yugoslavian military, my family and I were secluded in our home, as were all of our cousins in our village. Our village was then, and still is, surrounded by Serbian villages, and at that time a military base was just a mile away from our house. We weren't able to leave the house day and night while NATO bombs were shaking the ground; Serbs, on the other hand, were firing into our homes as an act of revenge.

It was April 15, 1999, when a group of armed Serbian soldiers surrounded our little village. They demanded money, gas and food. After threatening to kill us all, they took what they needed and warned us that they'd return in two hours. At that point, my father said, "We are leaving now." My parents, my siblings and I, within those twenty minutes we had, took our essential belongings and jumped into our car. I, of course, took my poetry notebook and hid it underneath my sweater. Three of my uncles and their families followed us, too. We took the highway, not knowing where we were going at all, but there was no hope to remain in our village. Halfway to town, we saw a Serbian soldier blocking our way and aiming his gun at us, getting ready to fire. We previously had been warned by some Serbs not to take the highway, but that was our only chance of escape. I remember my father saying, "If we stay, we die anyway, so let's try this last option," and we did. As Dad was driving slowly, straight towards the soldier, the soldier, on the other hand, was getting ready for his prey. We were all watching, stunned, waiting to get shot. All of a sudden, a voice rang out from the side, "Skender, Skender." My father's name was being called by a Serbian police officer who had known my father. As soon as the soldier heard his companion's call, he moved aside in confusion, lowered his gun, and let us go. Miraculously, we had escaped death from the hands of those who wanted to kill us.

From there, we went to a village a few miles away from ours and stayed at a cousin's house. Soon after we left our village, we heard the news the Serbs were burning our houses. I recall my memories of climbing up a wall and looking in the direction of my village where I had been born and had grown up. That day, April 16, every house in our village was robbed first, then set on fire. I could see the smoke going miles up in the sky, but I was able to do nothing. That was the only time in my life when I wished I could fly to see what was happening there. Sometimes I say I am glad I did not see anything but the smoke of my burning home.

Two weeks later, my family and I took the train to Macedonia. After that hard journey in a train packed with hundreds of people leaving Kosova, we settled in a refugee camp nearby Skopje (Alb. *Shkup*), the capital of Macedonia. Even there, I heard that some teachers and students had opened a school in a big tent. That sounded great to me. Living conditions were hard in camp but we were safe, at least. Just two weeks later, my family and I meet a group of volunteers from Italy who were inviting people to move temporarily to Sicily. Three days later, we left the camp with some other families and flew to Sicily.

As soon as we landed at the airport, I felt like we had arrived on a different planet. Our Italian hosts settled us in a former military base of Comiso. Within two weeks, Kosovar Albanian teachers opened a school there. It was nice to be back in school, even though in a completely different environment. The school was named "Jeronim De Rada" after a very well-know Albanian writer of the nineteenth century, whose works also had a great influence on my writings.

My family and I began a new life in Sicily; however, we were not alone. There were 6,000 other Kosovar Albanian refugees who had been brought from the Macedonian camps. While I went to school there, I also wrote numerous poems and began writing my life journey, what had happened and what was happening in Kosova at that time. Even though we were miles away from Kosova, my heart and mind were still there. I kept asking myself, "When will we return home?"

After a month of living in Comiso, my parents decided to move to Switzerland because we had a few cousins living there. I remember the day we left Comiso; I went to my class crying and told my classmates it was my last day to go to that school. It was time to say goodbye. On my way out of class, I taped a poem I had written a couple minutes before the class, dedicated to my classmates and my teachers, and ran out in sorrow, never to return again.

The following week, I was in Switzerland with my family. We were granted asylum there and settled in a neighborhood mostly populated with new settlers from Kosova and other countries around the world. While I was learning German and Italian there, I wrote a great number of poems and continued working on my life journal of my journey that seemed so long, despite the relatively short time it had taken.

On June 12, 1999, NATO forces entered Kosova. After so many years of struggle, Kosova was a free country and Kosovar Albanians were able to go back to their homeland. I still have the vivid images in my mind of the American and other U.N. troops entering Kosova, which appeared on TV, with Albanians celebrating around them. It certainly *was* something to be celebrated. My family and I were in Switzerland, but we immediately volunteered to return home, even though there was nothing left there that reminded us of home. In August, 1999, we were back in the village of our ancestors and began rebuilding everything that had been burned to the ground.

Shortly after our return, I resumed my education at the same school which, eight years prior, we Albanian children had been forced to leave in sorrow. Subsequently, I went to high school in my hometown, Lipjan, and, in 2002, I decided to finalize a long project that had followed me throughout my journey. I collected my favorite poems and drawings and published them in a long-awaited book named *Sfidat Jetike,* meaning *The Challenges of Life,* all in Albanian. I was eighteen at that time.

While I was in Kosova, I met a group of American missionaries who helped us rebuild our houses and provided food and clothing. I worked with them as an interpreter from the time I returned home. One of the families, the Offenbachers, invited me to come live with them and study in America. I certainly loved the idea, but there was a long way ahead of me to make that dream come true. I applied to

Rogue Community College in Medford, Oregon, and after spending almost two years studying English intensively for the TOEFL test required from every international student planning to study in the United States, I saw my dream come true.

*   *   *

By the fall of 2005, I was at Rogue Community College working on my AAOT degree with a focus in psychology. Since I came to America, I have come to realize I have learned to see the world in a different way. Interacting with people of various cultures, thoughts and beliefs, I strongly believe my perception about the rest of the world is tremendously changed. Also, giving speeches and presenting the history of my country and the culture to the students and the professors, both at Rogue Community College and Southern Oregon University and in the community, and comparing those experiences with other peoples', has greatly broadened my scope of understanding the world around me. Student questions and comments have made me think and learn things about my county, also, that I would never have thought about when I was in Kosova. As I progressed with my English, I began writing both in Albanian and English, especially poetry. My writings have found so much support from students, faculty members and teachers who read them in the college paper, *The Byline*; and those are some of the people who have encouraged me to write this book.

Education here in America, however, has had the greatest impact on my life. The rapid progress of psychology and its wide acceptance by the society here is just fascinating to me. Also, given the opportunity to read different types of writings from different authors from all over the world, I find that my vision of the past, present and the future has been greatly reshaped. Therefore, in this book, besides my past experiences in Kosova, I have combined various ideas, religious thoughts and philosophies into one book, making it a mixture of views that lead to one path, the universal unity of the people all over the globe. As a result of all these combinations, I decided to name my book *The Alchemy of Mind,* because I believe our reason can grasp and produce much more than we think. It can take all the good parts of different bodies, melt them all together and turn them into one pure body of "gold," light for enlightenment, that serves us in our everyday lives.

He who has health has hope, and he who has hope has everything.

—Arab Proverb[33]

Quotations, Inspirations and Other Notes

1   From *The Gift* of Hafiz, the Persian Sufi master. Translated by David Ladinsky and others. From thinkexist.com.

2   From the *Quotable Quotes* of Reader's Digest.

3   An inspiration from the writings of Morihei Ueshiba, founder of the popular Japanese martial art Aikido, that he called the Art of Peace. *The Art of Peace*. Translated by John Stevens. Shambhala Library.

4   Inspiration from *The Art of Peace*.

5   In amazement with the discoveries in the field of marine biology.

6   Inspired by the writings of the U.S. Sen. Al Gore, *Earth in the Balance*. Plume.

7   In fascination with Einstein's complex and genius works in the field of physics.

8   From Chekhov's *Misfortune*. Translated by Constance Garnett. From en.wikiquote.org.

9   Translation of the poem: Stuhite e Jetës from *Sfidat Jetike,* by Flamur Vehapi. BAF.

10 Translation of the poem: Edhe Unë from *Sfidat Jetike* by Flamur Vehapi. BAF. Adapted in English with some slight changes.

11 Revised. This poem was published on *The Byline*, Rogue Community College paper, March 2006 Medford, Oregon.

12 Quote from Moshe Dayan, politician from Israel.

13 Quote from the Baptist minister, Martin Luther King Jr. *Let the Freedom Ring.*

14 Adapted from Michel Montaigne, Essay *On Cannibals.* The Norton Anthology.

15 Dedicated to the bloodiest wars of the end of the 20th century in Bosnia and Kosova.

16 Martin Luther King Jr. quote.

17 Inspiration from Lao Tsu, Integrity from *Tao Te Ching* translated by Ralph A. Dale. Barnes & Noble Publishing.

[18]   From the *Quotable Quotes* of Reader's Digest.

[19]   Sura 22, verse 7 of the Qur'an.

[20]   Quote from Lao Tsu, Limitations from *Tao Te Ching* translated by Ralph A. Dale. Barnes & Noble Publishing.

[21]   From the *Quotable Quotes* of Reader's Digest.

[22]   Adapted from Lao Tsu, Who are you? *Tao Te Ching* translated by Ralph A. Dale. Barnes & Noble Publishing.

[23]   Adapted from *The Wisdom of Muhammad*. Citadel Press.

[24]   From Rumi, Union, *A Garden Beyond Paradise*. Translated by Jonathan Stark and Shahram Shiva. Bantam Books.

[25]   In appreciation of the work of Arbinger Institute in the *Leadership and Self-Deception*. BK.

[26]   Confucius Sayings from quotemountain.com.

[27]   From quoteworld.org.

[28]   Dedicated to the Seal of the Prophets.

[29]   Quote from the sayings of Jesus.

[30]   Quoted from *The Wisdom of Muhammad*. Citadel Press.

[31]   *Editor's Choice Award* winning poem.

[32]   From the *Quotable Quotes* of Reader's Digest.

[33]   From the *Quotable Quotes* of Reader's Digest.